A WAY WITH WORDS!

A SURVIVAL GUIDE AND NAVIGATIONAL TOOL IN THE FORM OF QUOTES AND PHRASES DESIGNED TO HELP MANEUVER LIFE'S

TURBULENT TIMES AND UNCERTAIN MOMENTS!

<u>Knowledge= Facts , information and skills acquired by a person through experience or education.</u>

1. Navigate by sight but live by faith.

2. Staying positive throughout the battle

makes the results of the war much more bearable.

3. Closing old chapters is the only way to open new book's and begin new adventures.

4. Never let the disappointment of not advancing stop you from performing at a high level.

5. Things don't always work as we plan but as long as they work out is all that matters in the end.

6. Race, color , creed don't determine good people actions do.

7. Things and people are usually better in their purest and most original form.

8. Whats unconventional to

them maybe conventional to you pave your own path.

9. Make sure you take full advantage of the position you are in before you get the position you want and request.

10. People opinions of you only matter when you give them value.

11. Be as humble in your wins as you are in your loses.

12. Learn from your mistakes and let them make you great.

13. Patience plus persistence is a simple formula for some of the most difficult equations.

14. Never worry about hurting a persons feelings in situations regarding or

related to survival ,safety or well being.

15. Apologise with actions not words.

16. Protecting those we love should be just as important as protecting ourselves.

17. The right time to do the right thing is right now.

18. Call me to compliment me just as much as you do to correct me.

19. Just because you want the best for a

person doesn't mean you know what's best for them.

20. No amount of money is more important then making sure family is straight and in a good place.

21. Not even family has the right to use you only when its convenient to them.

22. If it cost you your peace of mind, your sanity or safety its not worth it.

23. The destination is important but the journey is the portion of the experience you learn the most from.

24. Being the voice of reason can put you in a vulnerable position but the price of peace is priceless.

25. Our children want just as much for us as we want for them so leading by example is imperative to both our growths.

26. Sometimes failure presents our best opportunities not only

for who we are but also for who we are truly to become.

27. Self improvement is a endless journey with limitless rewards.

28. Hold yourself accountable and

responsible with the same scale you use for others.

29. Identifying opportunity when it presents itself is a skill taking advantage of those opportunities when the time comes is a gift.

30. Use the same level of humility in your wins as you do in your loses.

31. No matter how many people see your greatness you will never be able to

flourish until you see it for yourself.

32. Listen to learn and not to respond.

33. Some people only like, love and appreciate you when they are using you.

34. Sometimes what you have to do is the bridge or form of transportation that will get you to what you want to do.

35. The term friend should be used only when earned and requires constant

maintenance to be retained.

36. Learn as much from the failure of others as you do from the success.

37. The worst person in the world to ignore

or take for granted is father time.

38. The most simple tricks usually keep the crowd deceived and occupied the longest.

39. Some people extend help only to appear superior in the

face of there peers and on lookers.

40. Authenticity is a individual trait not a group disposition.

41. My insecurities from past experiences should not hinder my

ability to live fully and freely.

42. We can never master or correct our inadequacies if we constantly monitor those of others.

43. Passing judgment is a luxury designated

and delegated to those who have mastered the art of perfection.

44. Loving what you do and getting paid to do it is a luxury so many of us take for granted.

45. Even the most humble individuals like to hear thank you and I appreciate you every so often.

46. Change has many different meanings and purpose but positive change

should have the same intention.

47. Sometimes our short comings are not detectible until we see them projected through and from others.

48. The objective should be to surround ourselves with friends who only supply and support us with positive peer pressure.

49. Most people search for money and power but the true journey in life should

lead to meaning and purpose.

50. Knowledge is the fuel needed for the brain to not only create but problem solve at its highest level.

51. The easy route usually leads to a mediocre destination.

52. Confidence usually comes from the experience that failure brings.

53. Once we find passion for our

purpose casual and comfortable will no longer apply to our day to day lives.

54. People tend to ignore the process if the results equal success.

55. Believe in yourself ten times as

much as those who support you.

56. Only a fool would enter an open conversation with a closed mind.

57. Changing environment is key in changing perspective

that leads to mental growth and ultimately financial gains.

58. The ultimate confidence is best displayed within the confines of humility.

59. Sometimes the people we thought

where going to hold us down end up holding us back.

Insight. The power or act of seeing into a situation.

61. Some people don't have the capacity to appreciate or reciprocate your level of loyalty.

62. Its ok to revisit hard times in your life but try not to reside there.

63. Some of our best blessings come in the form of knowledge and opportunity not money and material.

64. One of the best feelings in the world is helping others find there gifts and or greatness.

65. Sometimes we have to disappear or remove ourselves to find ourselves.

66. Some people would rather fail then ask for or except help don't take it personal.

67. Once you begin to love yourself you will care less about who does and doesn't like you.

68. You will never reach your destination without proper direction.

69. If we convince ourselves something is to tedious or complicated sooner or later our minds will believe it.

70. Stop dreaming and start being.

71. The next person can give you the opportunity to succeed but the actual success is up to you.

72. The maintenance of certain relationships are important to your

growth and peace of
mind.

73. Make sure they
show you they love
you just as much or
more then they tell
you.

74. If you love me
don't bring me things

or people that could potentially do me harm or disturb my peace.

75. Every interaction is an opportunity to change someone's perception or perspective.

76. It's not what you do its how you do it and what you do with it.

77. Don't let the next person's journey or results dictate how you operate.

78. Plan and prepare for the future but maximizing the moment consist of living in the now.

79. Wanting success and working on success are two different things.

79. Prepare for hard times before they come so it won't be so uncomfortable when they arrive.

80. Don't let others or yourself convince you of what you can't do.

81. Do things to make your loved ones proud but don't forget to impress yourself in the process.

82. Proving someone wrong should never become more important then making the right

decision or getting the best results.

83. Asking questions and accepting assistance is a underrated attribute of the more intelligent.

84. Learn from your mistakes or moving

forward will become your biggest obstacle.

85. We complicate the simple things in life by ignoring the sign's right in front of our faces.

86. You should never have to belittle the

next individual to make yourself feel important or intelligent.

87. Finding information first is good but the ultimate goal should be passing it forward.

88. Blaming the next individual for your short coming's is sometimes more convenient then it is factual.

89. Learning from the mistakes of those we have loved and lost is

the best way to pay homage.

90. God knows your wants and worries but more importantly he knows what you need and deserve.

91. Never let your situation or

circumstance take away from your ability to count your blessings and see all the beautiful things life has to offer.

92. An apology can go a long way when it's genuine and from the heart.

93. Never force a person to appreciate what you bring to the table, the effort is from the heart and the appreciation is optional.

94. Finding the bad in people is easy finding the good is a gift.

95. If criticizing the next persons efforts is the only way you contribute to a cause maybe you are also apart of the problem.

96. Some people despise others success, because it reminds them of there lack of hard work and sacrifice.

97. What is common sense to you might be complicated to them be patient.

98. If helping the next individual steals your joy and disrupts your peace say no.

99. Sometimes the anger we show towards others is really disappointment we have for ourselves.

100. Ignoring and over looking responsibilities won't make them go away so its better to address them even when its stressful.

101. Navigation without direction will

never get you to your destination.

102. The next person's accomplishments are not your failures they are your inspiration.

103. It's not a bad thing to be corrected

when your wrong its actually a blessing.

104. Make being productive apart of your regular routine. 105. Even in our darkest moments we have a choice to be optimistic and positive.

106. Give your dreams room to breath and always feed you passion and your purpose.

107. Give people the space to make things right even in the midst of there mistakes.

108. The promotion of negativity usually invites and opens the door for bad energy.

109. Judge a person by their actions not by the next person's opinion of them.

110. Serious situations should never be addressed on social media or in the public for that matter.

111. Ignoring red flags, red lights, and or our instincts can not only be dangerous but also deadly.

112. Never get mad at a child for not knowing something you never taught them.

113. Disrespect is not a diagnosis it's a decision.

114. Some of your most turbulent times are only training you for your most triumphant ones.

115. Unconditional love is much more powerful and valuable then money and material.

116. Your sanctuary should include and incorporate your safety.

117. Serving our people should result in eternal life not lose of life.

118. Loyalty is something people learn from you not something they use when necessary.

119. Never try to navigate the next person's relationship.

120. Being alone is being absent of company being lonely is living with a person without communication and consideration.

121. Don't let your circumstances force you to do things you

should have done by choice.

122. Your past experiences influence your direction but do not have to determine your destination.

123. Don't let being in a relationship

become more important then being in the right relationship.

124. Real love requires protection and preservation.

125. Any product or person attached to the

word perfect is probably a prolific perpetrator.

126. If something or someone is a threat to your peace of mind keep it or them at a safe distance at all times.

127. Sometimes the reality we create in our minds is not the reality of the actual situation.

128. Never down play situations that deal with safety or survival.

129. The first step to gaining others respect is to show how much you respect yourself.

130. If the cost of making the next person happy is making you miserable the fee is too much.

131. After a while taking a person's kindness for weakness becomes instinctual not intentional.

132. Unfortunately some of the best things and people in our lives will not be valued and

appreciated until they are long gone.

133. Learn to live with the fact that you may not be everyone's cup of tea.

134. The elevator may be faster but the stairs make you stronger.

135. If you have anything to prove it is to yourself and no one else.

136. Once you find passion you will usually find your purpose.

<u>Understanding=</u>
<u>Sympathetically aware of</u>
<u>other peoples feelings.</u>

137. Some people test the boundaries of your relationship because they don't respect it.

138. Be happy for others like you want

them to be happy for you.

139. The best legacies are usually built organically.

140. The average individual will forfeit friendship for popularity.

141. Privacy is the best protection from the petty and pitiful.

142. Honor, appreciate and respect any person that puts in the effort to help you be better.

143. The most important step to all great achievements is getting started.

144. Let the world sleep on you but never sleep on yourself.

145. The best part of some of your favorite relationships has came and went.

146. Real friendship should never intentionally put you or your safety in jeopardy.

147. Trailblazers rarely use the conventional route.

148. Give credit to those who deserve it and take detailed notes of the process and there results.

149. A heart full of hate blocks blessings and deflects positive vibes and good energy.

150. No matter how much you love a person you could never live for them.

151. Make sure your friends and circle match your goals and your lifestyle.

152. No matter how talented you are sooner or later that talent will require hard work and

tenacity to reach the masses.

153. Sometimes showing up is just as important as winning.

154. Your expectations should incorporate and require elevation.

155. You can never reach your full potential living in your comfort zone.

156. When properly packaged and marketed your pain can be profitable.

157. Don't let traditional thinking confine your creative thought process.

158. When everyone around you thinks your not reaching your full potential believe them.

159. Don't let the misery and negative outlook of others spill over on to your plate of enthusiasm.

160. Hone in on your God given gifts and capitalize on your creativity.

161. Never let your potential out weigh or over shine your production.

162. Life doesn't stop while we go through our trials and tribulations.

163. Your success is your vehicle you decide the direction and destination.

164. A wise man once told me its always something to do.

165. Your dreams and your success are your responsibility.

166. Everyone is not worthy or receptive to your level of energy.

167. Lead with love and respect leave with honor and integrity.

168. For some people drama is there norm and chaos is there comfort zone.

169. You control you action not the next person's reaction.

170. Changing the way a person looks at you is your opportunity to change the way they look at the world.

171. If we are not careful arrogance and ego will outshine our

accomplishments every time.

172. The respect you give to others is a reflection of how you feel about yourself.

173. At some point we have to take responsibility for the

relationships we choose to participate in.

174. For some people living a lie is much easier then admitting they are wrong.

175. The next person's happiness is

not your job or responsibility.

176. The best relationships have lines and boundaries to keep the love and loyalty intact.

177. Be a student of your mistakes and of those around you.

178. Observe the actions and absorb the energy.

179. Reflect on past strength to get you

through today's exercise.

180. Sometimes you have to people tuff it out just so they know they can.

181. Small practices of discipline can turn into full blown habits

if implemented properly.

182. Following a successful blueprint is always good but creating your own is usually more lucrative.

183. Don't let words like family or love disable your common sense or basic instinct.

184. Selfish perspectives are not productive for team play.

185. Every challenge does not require conflict or confrontation.

186. Good friends never make you feel guilty about your growth.

187. Give your attention to things and people that make you better.

188. Some people only do things for us so they can tell people they did things for us.

189. Move without motives.

190. Giving up and moving forward are two different things.

191. Give your time to those who cherish it not just enjoy it.

192. Others opinions of you is more about there lives then they are about yours.

193. If you ever question what you can make it through take a look back at what you made it through.

194. Sometimes the advice we are giving is not the example we are living.

195. Passing judgment and putting you up on game can sound the same depending on the delivery.

196. Minding other peoples business is not a form of entertainment.

197. Living your best life should not include intentionally making the next person feel jealous or envious.

198. Always ask yourself what am I trying to achieve with my actions.

199. At some point living solely for yourself won't be enough to feed your purpose.

200. How we finish things is very important but the initial step is imperative.

201. Push yourself so your situation doesn't have to.

202. Convincing the public is easy; deceiving yourself is hard altering the reality is impossible.

203. Sometimes the thought of success can scare us more then that of failure.

204. Reflect on the pain so you can remember your purpose.

205. You inspire those around you even when you are not aware of your impact on there lives.

206. Mistakes will be made but reconciliation can be accomplished if the opportunity is given and the efforts are genuine.

207. Don't expect more from people

then you are willing or able to give.

208. Hopefully communication leads to compromise and conclusions we can live with and move forward from.

209. Understanding envy is the job of the envious.

210. Co pilot is a very important position especially in the flight through life choose wisely.

211. Inevitable changes sometimes require maximum flexibility.

212. Look for me in your good times with the same vigor you do in your hard times.

213. Never expect the next person to protect what's important to you.

214. The support usually only comes after they get the scent of your success.

215. Some of our biggest problems come from our lack of security in regards to our privacy.

216. Some of the most evil intentions and hidden agendas are camouflaged by

righteous causes and horrific tragedies.

217. Excepting or not addressing self destructive behavior can be the same as or worse then supporting it.

218. Your growing pains in the end should result in glorious gains.

219. Never let your ego put you in a loose loose situation.

220. New opportunities and

experiences can never fully blossom until we close old chapters and modify old behaviors.

221. Judgment and ridicule should be reserved for masters of perfection and no one is perfect.

222. Authenticity and stability last longer than popularity and publicity.

223. Keep waiting on your moment and your moment may never come.

224. Don't be offended by the truth be motivated.

225. Your day in the sun might come but the shine is sold separately.

226. Some people receive there big

break and others take the ultimate risk.

227. Inspire with your words but lead with your actions.

228. The word family can be used as a tool for master manipulation.

229. Remind yourself of the days of desperation so during the calm moments you don't become complacent.

230. Never pass up an opportunity to get better.

231. Using the word friend to loosely is a recipe for disappointment.

232. Goals and dreams are achieved not received.

233. Listen more and talk less.

234. Waiting for the right time is a tool of the master procrastinator.

235. Don't miss your fish watching the next person's pole.

236. Its hard finding solutions when we are busy pointing fingers.

237. Believe in your potential as much as those who love and support you.

238. Talent without ambition is like a race

car with no transmission.

239. Denying or debating the facts will not change the truth.

240. Perfect scenarios and situations are rare so we must learn to

perform in hostile environments.

241. The higher the horse the further the fall.

242. Why wait on a miracle when you can make one.

243. Reserve judgment for yourself you will benefit from it more then anyone else.

244. The only thing that separates you from those you respect and admire is effort.

245. Success, hard work and sacrifice are synonyms.

246. There intimidation of your attributes will not allow them to support you.

247. Who deserves success more then you?

248. You owe yourself much more then anyone else.

249. Lack of results is usually a bi product of lack of effort.

250. Finding purpose is one thing applying it is another.

251. Stop looking for people to blame and start looking for things to change.

252. Real friendship is like a art form it

takes constant practice to perfect it.

253. Don't forget to count your blessings while you are working on your dreams.

254. Stop giving people access to your

life that don't have your best interest at heart.

255. At some point we have to stop living for everyone else and start living for ourselves.

256. Listen to learn not to challenge or respond.

257. When the truth hurts you can either defend it, except it or change it.

258. Never expose your hand to the

opposition being unpredictable is an asset.

259. Your priorities and preferences are usually driven by your opportunities.

260. Sometimes its hard to admit or even

imagine that we are standing next to or in the presence of greatness.

261. Acknowledging the next persons potential or greatness is a testament to your maturity level and confidence.

262. We don't have to share the same opinion to respect each others position.

263. Often times we ignore the signs that help us dictate or decide who is real and or authentic.

KIU= KEEP IT UP.

264. If you love a person let them evolve how they see fit.

265. Your path should include what's best for you not friend's, family or society.

266. The more big loses you take the more little things you appreciate.

267. To some people the only hardships and problems that exist are the ones they

go through and encounter.

268. Take responsibility for your failures the same way you do for your accomplishments.

269. Sitting on potential will keep it

worm but never allow it to catch fire.

270. Be a student of your experiences.

271. Never ignore your instincts they are a cheat sheet to difficult decision making.

272. You have the right to defend yourself against any act of terrorism or intimidation.

273. Don't let your circumstances or situation turn you into a victim.

274. Delivering information properly can be just as important as delivering the proper information.

275. Surround yourself with individuals who want

to see you shine and succeed.

276. People can never assist you if they don't know you need help.

277. Making mistakes is common but choosing not to

address or correct those mistakes when given the opportunity is tragic.

278. No matter how you deliver the jewels some people will never receive the gift.

279. Sometimes the only way to get different results is to change your approach.

280. Its ok to help others with there dreams and goals as long as you don't forget about yours.

281. Words can be received much different then intended in delivery.

282. Some people's insecurities will never allow them to be proud of or root for you.

283. Sometimes your darkest moments bring out your best attributes.

284. Sometimes what we want and desire does not fulfill Gods expectations of us.

285. The weight that seems unbearable is the exercise you need to accomplish the unthinkable.

286. Sometimes we fight for those we love in the midst of them fighting against us.

287. Before we can ever get where we want to go its imperative we identify where we stand.

288. Some people are not ready to receive

your level of love and consideration.

289. What things are and what we want things to be are usually two different things.

290. Your biggest goals are usually

hidden behind doors that resemble your greatest fears.

291. The distance between where you are and your destiny is based on dedication and decision making.

292. Making our wrongs right is a full time job with no retirement.

293. Some equations can be solved by your self and others require reinforcements.

294. Conversations initiate changes but actions help implement them.

295. Most self improvement begins with sacrifice.

296. The best opportunity to bring

change in the immediate future are directly related to the messages we give to the children.

297. Negative thoughts never made a bad situation better.

298. Negativity and bad energy should be deflected not reflected.

299. In some situations faith is all we have but once we make it through we find out faith is all we needed.

300. Some of the smallest gestures to you mean the world to someone else.

301. Sometimes it's not about being right its about getting the right results.

302. Live in the moment not for the moment.

303. It takes a great person to assist others even in the midst of there own hardships.

304. The best way to honor those we lost is

to remember how they would want us to live.

305. Some individuals don't handle stress well don't hold it against them.

306. When people who know you

intimately are not included in your success they take it more personally.

307. If you love someone give them the space, opportunity and respect to have there own opinions.

308.
Accomplishments and accolades are great but your mark will be left in your message.

309. Your opinion and position on things that are not your business should not concern you.

310. Being right or correct does not void the common courtesy of listening.

311. Its hard to give a accurate assessment of something you can only see from a distance.

312. Even if we don't agree with a person celebrating wins should be left up to the individual.

313. The best way to salute the ones who came before you is to pave the way for the

ones that come after you.

314. Being bitter not only blocks your blessings but it also prevents you from getting better.

315. In a world full of followers, leading by

example can be the only way to awake the sheep from there sleep.

316. Some of the best information in the world was missed and overlooked because of the cover of the book.

317. For some people being ignorant is much easier then being enlightened.

318. Religious stance and political stance are usually more about programming then personal choice.

319. Loving a person intimately usually requires learning them intricately.

320. Strike a nerve and spark a flame.

321. Speak your truth not the truth that the

world has given to you.

322. When it's all said and done make sure you lived your life not the life others wanted for you.

323. We have to be real with ourselves

before we can be real with anyone else.

324. Its unfair to expect perfection from any human being.

325. Honor and integrity is in the

execution not the position.

326. Good deeds and kind gestures where made for paying forward not paying back.

327. Loyalty is not an inherited trait it's a learned behavior.

328. Implement subtle changes that lead to major improvements.

329. Some individuals use basic conversation

to obtain important information.

330. Hardships and hard times are the only things that humble hard heads.

331. The less you depend on people the

less they disappoint you.

332. Take people and things for what they are not for what you want them to be.

333. Sometimes we have to dig up our

roots to remember our purpose.

334. Never become victim of your own arrogance and or ego.

335. Sometimes changing perception requires changing direction.

336. Its hard to get mad at a person for asking you to or expecting you to keep your word.

337. If it's important to your survival do your homework and your research.

338. The reasons they choose to hate you or love you is totally up to them.

339. Never give up on what and who you love.

340. The worst thing you can do when you get up is forget who stayed down.

341. Unfortunately bad recommendations can be seen as bad judgments in character.

342. Dealing with everyone the same is optimistic but not realistic.

343. It is totally possible to have different belief systems but be on the same mission.

344. Separate yourself from those who don't have any or similar goals.

345. Find who and what is important to you and give them and it your undivided attention.

346. For some people acting like they don't want attention is there way of asking for it.

347. Diplomacy should always be the first choice but guerilla tactics should always be an option.

348. Good advice means nothing if you don't put it to use.

349. Save and sacrifice now so you can stunt and shine down the line.

350. Down talking or down playing the next

persons accomplishments is not an antidote for making you feel better about yourself.

351. Intimately understanding a persons perspective requires intricately

knowing their experiences.

352. Apologizing or admitting when your wrong can only make you better in the long run.

353. Believe in the ones who salute and

support you as much as you do in the ones who hate and ridicule you.

354. Being productive in the midst of the storm is just as important as being patient.

355. Check on and support those you love just as much as you would like them to do for you.

356. Before you can help a person get to the future you have to first help them get through the moment.

357. Not agreeing with a person is not a good enough reason not to listen.

358. Some people will never appreciate your presence until you make them feel your absence.

359. If you are only loyal and trustworthy when you are winning then you are not real.

360. If respect and common consideration is not reciprocated when requested then at some point it should

be required to move forward.

361. Only be responsive to energy that reenergizes your spirit and rejuvenates your soul.

362. Some people use humor to disguise the

hate don't be fooled or confused.

363. Real dreams and ambition require maintenance.

364. Real friends and family should bring joy to our lives not drama.

365. Family means don't worry about me, because I love you.

This book is dedicated to the memories of Linda Price, Glenda Woodward, Corine Price, Clinton Price, Calvin Price, Demtrieus Price, Geneva Harrison , Laura Price, Eural Price, Pearlie session and Andre Price.

This book is also dedicated to all the friends I lost to senseless violence in the savage streets of San Francisco California. Capone Thomas, Brandon Hollis, Kareem Sullivan, Lawrence Thomas, Marvel Despanie, Robert Bell, Montrell Harris, Matthew Byrd, Rahsaan Johnson just to name a few. I could never think of you all but this is for you and I love you!

Last but no least to my children Kaori, Jai and Akemi daddy loves you and although I fell you at times I hope you all know how much I love and learn from you everyday of my life, thank you.

To my biggest motivation of all, my soul mate, my best friend and my motivator my wife. You are the strongest most resilient human being I know and you have giving me the gift of fatherhood and taught me how to be a loving and more forgiving human being in the process. The strength, honor and integrity you operate with on a daily basis and the way you love is the stuff legends are made of. You inspire me to do and be better on a daily basis. I hope you know how deeply I love you and how thankful I am to God that he made you for me. Your journey and story is not and will not be in vein this is for you. Thank you for helping mold this boy into a man you are appreciated.

Made in the USA
San Bernardino, CA
15 June 2020